595.00

CW00829746

malawi
LAKE OF STARS

This book is for Ken Lowe

malaŵi

LAKE OF STARS

PHOTOGRAPHY BY FRANK JOHNSTON
TEXT BY VERA GARLAND

CENTRAL AFRICANA LIMITED
BLANTYRE
1993

First Published Blantyre, Malawi, October 1993
Second impression July 1995
© Central Africana Limited/Vera Garland

ISBN 99908 14 12 0

Designed by Monique Stansfield
Typesetting and colour reproduction by Unifoto
Printed by Creda Press

Contents

Preface

This book has been 'a long time coming'. Some of the colour photography goes back twenty-one years – when I was first struck by the beauty of one of the most scenic landscapes in Africa and the warmth of the people of Malawi.

While Lake Malawi remains something of a secret among tourists, perhaps because of the continued dearth of luxury hotels, it has been, and is, famed among travellers of all ages. They remember the sunsets at Cape Maclear, the welcome of the tea-rooms along its shores, the friendly waves of innumerable dugout fishermen.

This book is for all like them, who appreciate not the transient glamour of resorts elsewhere but the real sincerity and unspoiled beauty of a continent in transition.

Publication would simply not have happened without the promptings of my wife, Maria Inés, the encouragement of collaborator Vera Garland and her husband Peter, the interest and cooperation of the Malawi Department of Tourism, with whom I have cherished links, as well as the national airline, Air Malawi. Further prodding came from many friends, too numerous to mention, in Malawi and elsewhere in Southern Africa. Designer Monique Stansfield has still not visited Malawi but now knows the *Warm Heart of Africa* better than most who live there.

The production team at Unifoto, Cape Town, including the redoubtable Suraya, were subjected to considerable pressure to publish the book before yet another year passed and did so without murmur. Likewise my gratitude also goes to Heiner Lutzeyer and Creda Press, whose vast contributions to the improvement of printing skills in Africa remain to be more fully recorded .

Finally this book aims to repay, albeit in token manner, part of the debt which my family and I owe to Malawi and its people for the happiness they have brought us over the past 21 years. Thank you Malawi.

F.M.I.J.
Blantyre, Malawi
October 1993

Invitation to the lake

Come to a lake where eagles fly. Come to the wild north where mountains touch the water or to the gentler south where hills stand guard over villages and soft green flatlands are alive with birds. Marvel at baobabs growing their inexorable way through the centuries, or mourn the palm trees beheaded by palm wine drinkers.

Spend an evening at the lake when clouds of glory set the sky glowing until darkness swiftly falls, then sit on the still-warm sand and watch the moon rise with cool brilliance. See the sky grow thick with stars and tick off constellations you never saw before; see satellites go their lonely way through space and send a hasty wish on a shooting star.

Come for a blessing of pure, clear water and the warm sun to dry you. And if one morning the sun is missing and the lake looks sullen and forbidding, stay for the drama as rain veils the mountains on the other side then crosses the lake like a wall. Enjoy the crash of waves on the shore. Watch the canoes run for home. Suddenly it will be still again and the waves will become lapping-calm as the lake turns to silk and peace descends.

Is this a place of peace then? Now you can say so, though often it was a place of war. A place of rest maybe? Yes, there's rest for you, though many have laboured here. A place that history passed by? No. Rather a place shot through with history, footprints of a nation in the making.

But history made by men and concerning men came lately. We must go back further than that, to the times before the lake was created.

In the beginning

DEEP in the far reaches of geological time – maybe 100 million years ago – a strange world existed in what is now the far north of Malawi.

A green, flowerless mass of swamp and cycad, giant ferns and mosses, was inhabited by enormous dinosaurs, some of them sixty feet long and twenty feet high at the shoulder. Giant water tortoises paddled the swamps. Sharing that early world with these outlandish creatures was a more familiar variety of insects, the fore-runners of our butterflies, grasshoppers, roaches, dragon flies, scorpions and centipedes.

The appearance of man on earth was still more than 60 million years away when some major, ecological change signalled the end for these dinosaurs. Their bones were hidden away in pockets among the sandstones, marls and clays of the future, clues set by Nature and left to rest until the twentieth century, when man's quest for knowledge would lead to their discovery in the seventy-mile long dinosaur beds of the Karonga area.

The great rift

Time passed; thousands of ages, a celestial evening. As time evolved the bowl of the swamp became a small lake. Then came the mighty cataclysm that begat the Rift Valley.

The movements were violent in effect, but spasmodic in execution. Slowly but relentlessly the south of the romantically-named Gondwanaland sank; islands were broken from the main land mass. A rending and cracking heralded the faulting and folding, the warping and lowering, then eventually that reshaping of eastern Africa now known as the Great African Rift Valley.

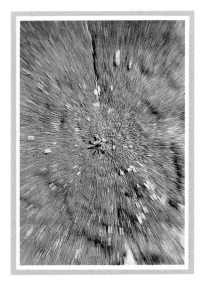

The prototype of Lake Malawi tipped, burst its southern banks and overflowed. Slowly the lake extended, helped by new faulting, and gradually the longitudinal trough of the rift was filled up. At first the lake was many metres – certainly more than 200 – higher than it is now, but by 2000 years ago it had more or less reached its present form.

16

▶ *The Rift develops*

◀ *Across the lake tower the Livingstone mountains of Tanzania*

▼ *The view of northern Lake Malawi from Livingstonia; Lulomo Peninsula shelters Young's Bay*

18

The lake that took shape

DISTURBANCES on the lake bed were ongoing, leading to earth tremors which occur up to the present day, while thermal springs appeared in some lakeshore areas. Yet the shape of the lake, its physical structure as we see it today, was now defined.

The landscape to the north of the lake forms a dramatic sight with the steep scarps of the Rift Valley dropping precipitously to lake level and continuing below, giving a record depth of 700 metres in some places.

Further south the western shore in particular has a more gentle aspect, with lakeshore plains and marshes softening the approach to the western Rift Valley edge.

Weather variations cause water spouts and also cause a tidal movement of the water and the broad expanse, combined with seasonal winds, gives rise to sudden storms.

There is apparently a regular long cycle of the rise and fall of Lake Malawi's waters, causing in turn a regular stream of theories seeking to explain the variation. Suggestions have included sunspot activity, deforestation, a natural tunnel connecting Lake Malawi with other large bodies of water, on-going geological faulting, natural gains and losses of water, sudd blocks on the Shire and so on. The mystery remains. Tips of steep hills, which were not quite overwhelmed by the Rift inundation, became islands. The isolation and smallness of most of these islands saved them from permanent human inhabitants and protected their vegetation, except for Likoma and Chizumulu, the largest, which are well-populated.

The lake coast has numerous peninsulas, points, spits and lagoons which form bays, although few provide good deep-water harbours.

This was the lake that developed, ready for creatures with more brain power than dinosaurs. The lake which had given shape to the land was now ready to shape history.

◄◄ *Water spouts are infrequently seen on the lake*

◄ *Likoma and Chisumulu Islands are the largest in the lake*

People at the lake

THE lake as a perennial water source meant life for man. Signs of early human occupation date back between 100,000 and 50,000 years and, according to artifacts found there, the Karonga area, home to the dinosaurs, was home also to some of the earliest men in Malawi. Here too was found a site with elephant bones and early tools, indicating a place where elephants were killed and butchered.

Remains of the Middle and Late Stone Ages have been found near the lake at Nkhata Bay, Nkhotakota and the Karonga area. Late Stone Age artifacts have also been found at Nkhunguni Hill in the Cape Maclear area.

Malawi moved into the Iron Age some 1800 years ago and by this time lake history had become more defined with the arrival of the Akafula.

The Akafula

Through legend and oral history we gather that the Akafula stemmed from a mixture of equatorial pygmy and wandering Khoisan. They were small-bodied people with large heads and some of the men had long beards. Apart from their short stature, leading to a "little man syndrome" (always wanting to have been seen from afar, thus proving they were big), they had many assets – excellent eyesight, good hunting skills and eventually the knowledge of how to work iron.

They came to the lake when there was an abundance of animals and fish and had time to develop their creative skills of rock-painting, pottery, song and dance .

With a plentiful supply of water and ample food, they perhaps led something of an Arcadian existence, which lasted until the sixteenth century, when their world finally fell apart.

The Amaravi

The Akafula met their nemesis in the Maravi people, who migrated from what is now southeast Zaire between the 13th and 16th centuries.

They were a war-like people, who eventually saw to the demise of the Akafula, though pockets of the Akafula, or Batwa as the Bantu called them, survived until less than two hundred years ago. This remnant gave rise to many legends. Even today there is a strong belief that some Batwa still live on Mchesi Mountain near Mulanje.

The Maravi people, coming from the north and west, were a collection of clans under one paramount chief. They arrived at the southern end of the lake where they built their capital. The land around became the Kingdom of Maravi. By the mid-seventeenth century the lake, known severally by previous map-makers as Zaflan, Zambre and Hemozura, was now named on some maps as Lake Maravi.

Maravi means "flames of fire". Many suggestions have been made to explain the origin of such a name: the rising or setting sun glinting on the lake? The glow from iron kilns? The ability to work iron? The most convincing theory (advanced by Dr. M. Schoffeleers) is that fire was a symbol of authority and power; a sign of transition, as in the burning of huts when one chief dies and another takes over; and a token of power in myths concerning God and man.

Certainly we know that the Maravi Empire was powerful and encompassed a time of transition as the clans spread out and colonised and, incidentally, established the ruling dynasty of the Chewa people.

Other incomers

The lake was big, and attractive to many other people. Between the fourteenth and sixteenth centuries the Tumbuka came from the northwest to Jenjewe Mountain, near Nkhata Bay, and the Tumbuka-Phoka people moved down around the Nyika area. Some time between 1550 and 1650 the Ngulube migrated from what is now Tanzania, round the northern end of the lake and into the Karonga area.

The eighteenth century brought further migrations. From around 1720-1780 the Balowoka came from the northeastern lake area and crossed the lake to Karonga, Chitipa, Rumphi and Nkhata Bay. They originally came to trade but decided to stay.

◀ *A graphic nineteenth century depiction of the horrors of Central African slavery*

During the nineteenth century the Angoni arrived and the Yao moved from Yao Hill in Mozambique and became established round the southern lakeshore.

By the mid-nineteenth century Swahili Arabs, attracted by ivory and slave trading, moved inland and set themselves up at places such as Mponda's, Nkhotakota and Karonga.

What had been a lake crossroads became a meeting point of many peoples; a place of confrontation.

The Amaravi, attacked by illness and declining in power and initiative, were unable to fend off the opposition. The rhythm of village life – the organised tribal life of planting and harvest, story and dance, initiation and celebration – was almost destroyed as the orderliness of central power disappeared and gave way to a life riddled with fighting and the fear of slavery or death.

Smartly, as if on cue, enter David Livingstone.

◀ *David Livingstone, from an 1866 engraving*

25

AFRICA.

BY JOHN CARY.

26

The big lake to the north

Maps prior to Livingstone's expeditions were based on sketchy reports from Portuguese traders. James Stewart C.E. published the first accurate maps in 1879

FOR centuries Europeans had speculated about the existence of a great lake in Central Africa, basing their imaginings on Ptolemy's second century map. In 1616 Gaspar Bocarro, travelling from Tete to Kilwa, crossed the Rift Valley in the vicinity of southern Lake Malawi. Travellers in the 17th and 18th centuries gave descriptions of the lake they had heard about and, in some cases, seen. Cartographers such as de L'Isle and d'Anville began to produce maps with the shape and position of the lake fairly accurately portrayed.

When David Livingstone visited Tete in 1856 he talked to Candido Cardoso who said he had visited the lake ten years earlier. Cardoso drew a sketch map of the lake, which Livingstone annotated. In later years Livingstone sought to discredit Cardoso's map and cast doubts on Cardoso's word that he had visited the lake.

Livingstone's own journey of exploration to the lake was something of an afterthought, a diversion from his original but thwarted plan to explore a way up the Zambesi River. The journey up the Shire River and the discovery of the lake mollified his disappointment over finding his Zambesi route blocked by the Kebrabasa Rapids.

While Livingstone was heading for the lake from the south, a young German, Albrecht Roscher, was struggling against malaria in Kilwa as he tried to raise a caravan of porters to head for the east coast of the lake.

In fact Roscher reached the lake only two months after Livingstone. He stayed there for a few months and then was murdered on a journey to the Rovuma.

It is tempting to speculate how history may have been changed if Roscher had been the first to arrive; interesting to imagine, had Roscher lived, how he and Livingstone might have interacted.

To Livingstone, however, goes the honour of "discovering" the lake – Lake of Stars, Lake of Storms, Lake Nyasa – and the word "discover" is used deliberately. For though the lake was known to Africans since the dawn of man there, and though Livingstone was almost certainly not the first European to see the lake, he was nevertheless the man who exposed it. After sailing on it, walking by it, meeting its people and suffering its storms, he made it known to the rest of the world.

It was two years after Livingstone's initial arrival at the lake before he set out to explore it. He travelled by boat and on foot up the west coast to the Nkhata Bay area and thought he had almost reached the northern shore of the lake. He was then forced by lack of food and time to go back to the Shire River.

He returned with notebooks full of information. In true Livingstone manner he details his observations of the lake and its people, telling us about length and depth, coast line and agriculture, boats and fishing, climate and health, trade and slavery. Nothing is thought too trivial to record and to Livingstone goes the credit for not only travelling the lake but also describing this lake-world to us as he found it in 1861.

On previous African journeys Livingstone had seen something of the slave-trade which was eating at Africa's gut. Now he saw evidence that thousands of slaves were being transported over the lake each year, to be sold – if they survived so long – in the slave markets of East Africa.

◄◄ *Albrecht Roscher – young, enthusiastic and vulnerable*

◄ *A late Victorian colour engraving of the missionary doctor*

▲ *Publishers of the time were not slow to portray the excitement of Livingstone's travels in 'darkest Africa'*

He had already begged for missionaries to bring Christianity to Central Africa. He now reasoned that a gun-boat on Lake Nyasa and an alternative trade to that in human beings would, together with Christianity, put an end to the slave trade.

His plea was answered and caused another change of direction in Malawi's history.

▶ *The billowing sails of dhows no longer foretell misery. Very few are now left, occasionally ferrying people and goods across the lake at its narrowest point near Salima*

▲ Livingstonia, photographed at Cape Maclear in 1891

▶ The same two baobabs photographed one hundred years later

Bibles, medicine and the ABC

THE first answer to David Livingstone's plea was provided by a group of Anglican missionaries who went to the Shire Highlands in 1861. Their tribulations, failure and eventual retreat to Zanzibar are fairly well documented .

After they left, twelve years elapsed before Livingstone's death inspired the Free and Established Churches of Scotland to send two parties of missionaries, one of which settled in the Shire Highlands, the site of present day Blantyre, and the other of which headed for the lake.

The Livingstonia Mission

In October 1875 the Free Church of Scotland group settled at Cape Maclear, a place on the lakeshore noted by Livingstone as a good harbour and which Livingstone had named after his friend Sir Thomas Maclear, Astronomer Royal at the Cape Town observatory.

The missionaries called themselves the Livingstonia Mission and set about planning their settlement. They laid the grounds out in a Union Jack pattern with gravel-covered walks in between the sections. By 1877 they had sixteen buildings in a row behind the "Union Jack" and parallel to the lake. Gardens were laid out for vegetable growing and a wooden fort was built in case of attack. They sought to dismiss ill-health by increased activity.

Dr Robert Laws began medical work, performing an operation on a patient on the dining table, using chloroform for the first time in this country. The teaching of Religious Knowledge, English and Mathematics was also started.

One task completed soon after the original mission party had arrived was the circumnavigation of the lake by Lieutenant Edward D Young, Dr Laws and three other missionaries on the *Ilala*.

◄ *The Ilala, transported as numbered packages, built and sailed on the Lower Shire, carried around the cataracts, then re-assembled on the Upper Shire, was the first steamship on the lake.*

▲ *A panoramic sketch showing the first British settlement at the Lake in 1879*

Edward D Young is a relatively unsung hero of the lake. He first travelled to this area as a member of Livingstone's Zambesi Expedition, commanding the *Pioneer* and *Lady Nyassa*. In 1866 Livingstone was reported missing and dead on his last journey near the lake and in 1867 Young was chosen to lead a search expedition. Livingstone, in fact, was still alive and had left this country. Young described his own adventures in an 1868 book called "*The Search after Livingstone*".

When the Scottish Church needed a leader for its Livingstonia Mission, Young was the obvious choice. Dr Laws was second in command and was affectionately referred to by Young as "*my boy*". The *Ilala*, the mission boat used for the circumnavigation, was the first boat with an engine to appear on the lake and people on the shore "*were paralysed with wonder as the 'big iron canoe', the first 'fireship' without oars or sails ... snorted past their villages*".

The mission journey round the lake enhanced Livingstone's discoveries and descriptions. Dr. Laws appears to have taken most of the observations. They found that the lake was 360 miles long, 160 miles longer than Livingstone had earlier estimated. They discovered at least 15 different tribes living on the shores of the lake, each with separate customs and languages.

They noted the amount of big game and saw for themselves the extent of the slave-trade which, by God's grace, they intended to stamp out. A later circumnavigation by James Stewart C.E. produced the first accurate map of the lake.

In October 1876 a further party of missionaries arrived. From the time of their arrival sickness prevailed. The fair aspect of the lake was blighted for the missionaries by the

◄ *The view over the lake from the Stone House, Livingstonia*

► *The stained glass window at Livingstonia shows Livingstone meeting the lakeshore chiefs*

▼ *Bandawe Old Church, newly restored*

low marshland near the mission with its lethal malaria-carrying mosquitoes. Livingstone came within a hair's breadth of connecting the presence of mosquitoes with malaria. Had he done so, the whole history and geography of early settlements might have been changed.

In addition to fears about the healthiness of the site, there was not enough arable land for the mission and so in 1881 the missionaries decided to move to Bandawe, still on the lakeshore but much further north.

The Livingstonia Mission kept its name when it moved to Bandawe and again in 1894 when it finally moved to Khondowe. This time the mission was not on the lakeshore but on a high plateau, where they found growing *"wild brambles, raspberries, cranberries and junipers"*. The move to Khondowe was made because Dr Laws and his co-workers realised the need for some kind of institution where Africans could be trained to cope with the growing need for industrial workers, medical helpers, pastors and, particularly, teachers. Khondowe they found to be an almost ideal place for their institution. The higher altitude was healthier and had a climate more conducive to hard work; it was still near the lake for easy communications; it had a fair water supply and a good wood supply and the sparse population enabled the Mission to acquire a big acreage of land for growing crops. In fact the success of Livingstonia was not to come from farming, because by the 1920s they had experienced failures in planned export crops as well as in food crops for their own consumption. Science became an early focus of their efforts.

In 1925 Robert Laws described how science became *"the handmaid of Christianity"*. The steam engine of the *Ilala* was the introduction, closely followed by hydro-electricity bringing power to the Overtoun Institute to enable the saving of wood and grinding of grain and to provide piped water and electrical light. A waggon road was laid up what seemed an impossibly steep path from the lakeshore and a printing press clattered away, enhancing the spoken word of Good News.

The training of Africans was a priority. By 1899 the school had over 230 pupils taking a full time course. In addition to this there were 25 people being trained as teachers, 2 studying a theology course and about a hundred apprentices and out-workers taking evening classes. Trained telegraphists were already working.

With such large numbers in training and only a small expatriate staff, great emphasis was placed on the pupil-teacher system. In 1902 thirty-six trained teachers graduated and some students went on to do specialised courses.

The institution continues its educational and medical work up on the high plateau, away from, but still in sight of the lake on which it was born.

Here it stays to this day celebrating in 1994 one hundred years of service to the nation.

◄ *Looking down on Livingstonia and the lakeshore from the 2500 m heights of the Nyika plateau*

▲ *The nineteen bends of the Gorode escarpment road to Livingstonia, an early feat of missionary engineering skill*

42

The Universities' Mission to Central Africa

IN 1863, after failure in the Shire Highlands, the UMCA retreated to Zanzibar to lick its wounds. Soon it began to expand on the East African mainland and eventually a Bishop was appointed who felt inspired to make a second sortie to Central Africa.

In 1881 Rev. William P. Johnson came overland from Zanzibar to the eastern lakeshore. He returned the next year with Rev. Charles Janson who died soon after they reached the lake.

Johnson decided that the best means of evangelising the village settlements on the lakeshore would be to use a boat as a floating mission station. By 1885 the boat, the *Charles Janson*, was ready for its educative work and Bishop Smythies negotiated with Chief Chitesi for a site on the island of Likoma.

"Likoma" means beautiful, pleasant or desirable. The name may have referred to its appearance or to the fact that it was a refuge safe from marauders. The actual site of the mission was called *Chipyela*, meaning "a place of burning", so named because that was where witches were burned.

Likoma Cathedral, unlike its predecessors which were built as temporary churches, was built to last. The Bishop, called it *"an outward sign of our having reached a position beyond that of pioneers. Its vastness looks forward. Its massive construction preaches permanence."*

The bricks were made mostly on the main land because there was not enough firewood to spare on the island for burning bricks. The building wood was also brought from the mainland, *"the best timber in all the country around".* Apart from what was pushed on a small trolley, all transportation on land was by headload – stone, brick, timber, iron and cement.

When the Cathedral was finished it was the justification of many years' work on the Island – spiritual, educational and medical – and of the prayers and lives (and deaths) of many missionaries.

◀ *The s.s.* Charles Janson. *The graceful steamer was launched ten years after the* Ilala *and worked on the lake until 1950*

◀◀ *Chisumulu and Likoma Islands lie close to the Mocambican shore*

◀ *Likoma Island cathedral*

▼ *"It preaches permanence"*

With the *Charles Janson* (named in memory of the dead priest) as supply and transport boat, this island fastness became the diocesan headquarters and shortly after the turn of the century, a large cathedral was built there. Who but Victorian Englishmen would have had the temerity to build a cathedral on an island in an enormous lake in Africa?

It was probably years before supporters at home fully appreciated the situation. One of the lady missionaries said, *"People at home often assume that our lake is some sort of Derwentwater."*

UMCA missionaries lived a fairly communal life. Only unmarried people were accepted after the very early days. They each had their own hut but always ate together. Board and lodging were free and a small amount of pocket money was allowed.

Life without family support could be lonely, particularly on outstations that were meagrely staffed. Animals became important as pets, not just cats and dogs, but more unusual and probably less friendly ones, such as Miss Fielding's scaly ant-eater!

Teaching, nursing, ministering and housekeeping were all full-time jobs, with little time left in which to mope. Holidays for Holy Days were often celebrated by having picnics or magic lantern shows while one Christmas at Likoma, *"After dinner we all went young and foolish and played games."*

As with the Scottish mission sickness and death, especially in the early years, were the norm rather than the exception. Many missionaries died in their first years at the lake. On the other hand, those who survived a few years were instilled with some kind of inbuilt toughness. Some missionaries stayed working at the lake for years, including Dr Laws, who served from 1875 to 1927 when he retired to Scotland and Archdeacon Johnson who stayed there until he died in 1928.

The growth of the Anglican lakeside church, using first the *Charles Janson* and later the legendary *Chauncy Maples* as floating mission stations is well known. Sadly, what was tolerably cheap to achieve at the beginning of the century was financially impossible by mid-century. The *Chauncy Maples* was sold and the diocesan headquarters were moved, first to Mponda's on the southern lakeshore, and then to Malosa, closer to Zomba.

Left behind was a strong lakeside church rather than a set of mission stations, and a thriving Anglican community on Likoma Island, where the old cathedral is still used more as a place of worship than as a beautiful anachronism for sightseers to admire.

▼ *The m.v.* Chauncy Maples, *burnished by the rising sun*

▶ *The ruins of an early mosque at Nkhotakota, centre of Islamic, and Anglican, influence on the lakeshore*

Missionaries of Africa

A third mission sought to become established at the lake in 1889, this time by the Roman Catholic Church. At the end of that year four "Missionaries of Africa", usually called "White Fathers", arrived at Mponda's in the hope of setting up the first foundation of the newly-formed Provicariate of Nyasa. They jumped into the 'deep end' of a ghastly situation and their daily records are witness to the death and destruction which attended the family affairs, struggles for succession, the slavery and war that surrounded them.

For a year and a half they 'trod water'; not building churches, not converting people, simply being there in faith. In June 1891 they were withdrawn. As so often happens in mission history apparent failure was not final failure. In 1901 the White Fathers returned and now, ninety years later, the lakeshore parishes are strongly established and thriving.

Islam

The proliferation of mosques in the lakeshore areas reminds us that Christianity was not the only outside religion to become established at the lake.

As Livingstone and Kirk approached the lake area they heard of people who lived there who did not eat pork, and of boats with sails.

Swahili traders who settled on the western lakeshore and Yao traders who visited the coast of East Africa brought many new ideas. By the 1870's Chief Makanjila had converted to Islam and soon he had a *mwalimu* in his area teaching reading and the Koran.

In 1885 Makanjila Village, with its three to four thousand people, had become almost a replica of an East African coastal community. Many people spoke Swahili and their square houses, some with carved door posts and lintels, their adoption of the *kanzu* as a form of dress, their use of *dhows* for lake transport and the growing of crops like coconuts and mangoes, all showed how much effect Islam had, culturally as well as spiritually. This inter-twining of culture and religion strengthened Islam into a formidable rival to Christianity.

▲ *An early ALC trading settlement*

▶ *Fred Moir, co-founder of the ALC, photographed in 1885*

Calico, beads, ivory & guns

With foresight engendered by necessity, the Livingstonia missionaries had brought with them the *Ilala* to serve as a life-line for transport, personnel and stores. Like Livingstone, they soon realised the need for an establishment concerned solely with trade, which would deal in commodities other than people, and at the same time, import goods needed by the mission and build up a travel service from the Zambesi to the Lake.

It was for these reasons that the Moir brothers set up the Livingstonia Central African Trading Company, later known as the African Lakes Company (the lakes referred to being Nyasa and Tanganyika), and afterwards known as the African Lakes Corporation, or ALC.

The main business started in Blantyre in 1878 but quickly spread to cover the areas in the north, including parts of the lakeshore.

For centuries before Europeans arrived, a network of trading routes had been built up with much traffic in textiles, beads, and metal work. There was a lot of trade with East Africa, often using ivory in return for goods. Eventually slaves had become the focus of this trade, providing a means of transport that could also be sold, along with the ivory they carried, at the East Coast.

In the second half of the nineteenth century there was a growing demand for "fire power". It is estimated that by 1882 the Jumbe of Kota Kota, a Zanzibari, had amassed two thousand firearms.

When the ALC began trading they had a ready market for gunpowder as well as calico, and in return they took ivory. They dealt with African and Arab alike and even at times with slave dealers, shipping huge quantities of tusks down the lake and out of the country. Though the management of the ALC had altruistic aims, recruitment often turned up irresponsible layabouts and there were complaints about bad behaviour to subordinates. Harry Johnston scathingly referred to the ALC as *"that miserable grocery business"*.

Nevertheless at the Karonga ALC station, which opened in 1884, affairs prospered at first as they traded with the Ngonde people and with Mlozi. Mlozi was of Arab descent and, after trading in the Luangwa Valley area, he arrived and built a stockade in the Karonga district about the same time the ALC set up their trading store.

Peace could not reign for long because Mlozi and the ALC both wanted to corner the ivory trade in the area, with the additional aim on Mlozi's part of making Karonga a sort of clearing and forwarding base for captured slaves.

In 1887 matters came to a head and hostilities broke out between Mlozi and the ALC.

▲ *Mlozi and his bodyguard*

◄ *An ivory store at ALC's Mandala Headquarters. By 1899 ivory accounted for only 6% of exports from the fledgling Protectorate*

▲ *After the battle at Karonga*

▶ *A caravan on the Stevenson Road*

52

Low Monteith Fotheringham, who was then in charge of ALC Karonga, quickly and wisely sent for reinforcements. Mlozi slowly and foolishly waited until reinforcements arrived and fortifications were built before he attacked. With additional forces recruited by the ALC from local spearmen a counter-attack was made and the hostilities came to a temporary halt.

Unsuccessful attempts were made to negotiate with Mlozi. Further attacks and counter-attacks took place; people were wounded and killed: a gun was purchased by the Nyasa Anti-Slavery Defence Fund, but had little effect. There seemed no end in sight. Neither side was able to win; neither side was willing to lose.

▲ *Fort Johnston, now Mangochi, was the centre of lakeshore trading effort*

► *Sir Harry Johnston, administrator extra-ordinary, writer and artist*

In 1889 Harry Johnston arrived in Blantyre as the new Consul. He travelled to Karonga and a peace treaty was made with Mlozi. British administration was about to begin.

Taxes, licences and soldiers

THE treaty with Mlozi was one of many made by Harry Johnston while on an expedition the length of the lake. He visited the lake missions, gaining advice and backing from the missionaries, and made agreements with the most important chiefs and leaders. The agreements ensured peace between Queen Victoria and the chiefs while gaining permission for British subjects to enter the chiefs' areas. The leaders also promised to obtain British consent before ceding any territory to foreign powers. The Portuguese had been casting envious eyes northward. The scramble for Africa was on the way.

By 1891 British interests in Central Africa were such as to need official designation and by May 14th of that year the country became a British Protectorate. Now the mills of colonial government began to grind.

Administration needs money – money for an army, money for gunboats, money for roads, a postal service and buildings. To assure some of the regular income needed, taxation was introduced, first as a poll-tax, then when that was not successful, as a hut tax.

◄ *Sikh soldiers were central to the Protectorate's efforts to eliminate slavery*

▲ *The essential pioneer – Hugh Charlie Marshall, Collector of Revenue, Customs Officer and Postmaster, Chiromo, 1891*

With taxes due, people had to find paid employment. Many people went down from the lakeshore areas to Blantyre and the South, where jobs were easier to find.

One of the first tasks of the administration was to rid the land of slavery. Sikh and Zanzibari soldiers were imported. Because the lake was in the front line of slave traffic, forts were built on or near its shores: Fort Johnston, Fort Maguire and Fort Mangochi, for example.

The sight of soldiers became familiar. The Sikhs wore black jackets with yellow braiding, white shirts, yellow trousers with gaiters, and black puggarees. Black, white and yellow were Harry Johnston's choice of official colours for the Protectorate, intended to indicate the different races working together. Even the government stationery was edged with a black, white and yellow border and had matching ribbons to join papers together.

For some years a kind of peace hovered over Karonga but by 1895 there were reports of raids and harassment by Mlozi and his followers. Harry Johnston tried one last time to negotiate with Mlozi but was spurned. Mlozi started to rebuild his stockade. It was imperative now that government should attack and win.

◀ *The exponents of slavery; a band of 'ruga-ruga' photographed in Mlozi's stockade*

◀ *The victims of slavery on the northern lakeshore were the peaceful Ngonde, whose hut building skills attracted much admiration from European visitors*

No chances were taken this time. A large force of men, well armed and experienced, besieged Mlozi's stockade. After a long attack with their one artillery piece they finally hit Mlozi's house. This was the signal for his forces to scatter, while Mlozi himself was caught, tried and hung.

For the next nineteen years there was something approaching peace at Karonga.

Skirmishing continued in other areas in the vicinity of the lake. The Yao led by Zarafi in the south-east of the lake still made spasmodic attacks and took prisoners. Chief Mponda also caused trouble and the Angoni needed pacifying. Some of the original forts needed rebuilding and slaves were still turning up to be officially freed: *"Captain Stewart has issued freedom papers to 142 slaves ... who have settled down in the vicinity of Fort Maguire"*.

By 1896 the road between Fort Maguire and Fort Johnston was pronounced *"perfectly safe"*. Gun boats made regular patrols around the lake.

◄ *A sand-spit off the beaches of Nkhotakota, the most important central lakeshore settlement*

▲ *The gun-boat* Pioneer. *Built at old Fort Johnston, she served, along with her sister-ship the* Adventure, *in the fight against the slave trade*

When Harry Johnston left for Britain in 1896, Alfred Sharpe became Deputy Commissioner and later Consul-Commissioner. By this time Johnston had persuaded the British Government to finance British Central Africa, replacing the British South Africa Company, who had done so previously. Indeed during the five years of Johnston's administration the British Government contributed some £64,000. The Protectorate was surveyed and its boundaries fixed, and the Cape to Cairo telegraph line marched on towards its lakeshore route. New *bomas*, centres of government administration in East and Central Africa, were built and new barracks and roads were planned to carry the increase in traffic which came from the growth in imports and exports.

Alfred Sharpe continued steadily with this work. He wrote a set of labour rules and insisted on game licences because he feared elephants would become extinct if not guarded by law. Ivory still left the country in great amounts – *"he had 120 loads of ivory, some of the tusks being over 180 lbs."*.

Customs stations were built and a hut tax of three shillings enforced in new areas, although people on Likoma Island were exempt so that they wouldn't desert the mission by going away to find work. In North Nyasa District people earned tax money by working as carriers on the Stevenson Road to Lake Tanganyika, getting eight shillings for a ten day trip.

◄ *Sir Alfred Sharpe, administrator, hunter and conservationist*

▼ *"All I need is a steady shoulder..."*
Hunting was not only for sport but, in the lives of the early residents, for the pot too.

At Kota Kota A.J.Swann, the Collector (of Taxes), urged people to grow rice for sale to earn tax money. This they did and in a few years it was being sold for 8 pounds per ton. *"The Kota Kota people are willingly bringing in their hut tax"* reported the Central African Gazette. In 1896 when Alfred Sharpe visited the area he found small red flags flying from many of the huts and being carried by many people. He learned that this meant they had paid their hut tax.

By the end of the century coinage began to be used as well as barter goods. *"At lake ports such as Kota Kota, Bandawe and even Karonga, English silver coinage is now thoroughly understood and asked for."*

Health problems leading to sickness and death sometimes sapped the power of the administration and people sent from England were not always of a suitably high calibre to withstand the rough and lonely life. Hard drinking and bouts of depression were often the result. For others, however, the lonely, uncertain life, with its immense responsibilities was extremely fulfilling.

Hunting was a popular relaxation, reflected by advertisements. Deuss and Kahn at Fort Johnston had "Green Tents, 7ft x 7ft with fly, machila and umbrella only £11 each - *especially convenient for short shooting trips, being an easy load for one man."*

A. J. Swann was the kind of Collector who took pride in his work. After his success with tax collecting at Kota Kota, he turned to improvement of amenities. It was felt a lighthouse would be useful so the enterprising Mr. Swann personally collected subscriptions locally and had a lamp erected on the end of the sand spit at a 25ft elevation. *"A lamp was purchased in Blantyre which burns all night without trimming; in fact it is an old street lamp."* People familiar with Blantyre's history will recall that Blantyre Town Council

bought street lamps for the town which were not a success, so the lamps were sold. It may well be the Kota Kota lamp was one of these. In any case it seemed to work well; we are told it could be seen on a clear night for a distance of six miles.

The army, built on the original core of Sikhs and Zanzibaris, developed quickly and soon Tonga and Yao men were recruited. The army was used to subdue trouble-makers in the Protectorate and experience gained at the lake was useful when soldiers were sent to fight abroad. In 1900 they were the *"first African battalion sent to Somaliland against the Mad Mullah"*. They were also sent to West Africa on the Ashanti Expedition, where they earned much praise: *"best drilled, best disciplined and best shooting"*. It was a high reputation for future soldiers to live up to.

Between 1904 and 1909 a road was made from Matope in the south right up the middle of the country to the north. It was the only land route to the "forgotten north" But the north, especially Karonga, would soon be in the news again.

◄ *Zomba Mountain makes an incongruous back-drop for the Naval Brigade in 1902*

▲ *The now tranquil shores of the lake near Karonga*

▶ *The* Guendolen *was the largest vessel on the lake until the modern diesel powered ships. After her wartime adventures, she stayed in government service until 1944*

The Lake in World War I

WITH a speed never seen here before – and probably rarely seen since – Nyasaland became embroiled in World War One.

In what is now acknowledged to be the first naval action of that war, Nyasaland struck a decisive blow. *"Naval Victory on Lake Nyasa"* proclaimed the Times of London and no doubt readers imagined boats armed to the gunwales firing broadsides at each other. In fact it was a fairly one-sided affair. The German gun boat *Hermann von Wissman*, originally an anti-slavery boat, was harboured at Sphinxhafen in what was then German East Africa. At the very outbreak of war, the *Guendolen*, a Nyasaland Government boat, sped to Sphinxhafen and there found the *Wissmann* hauled out of the water on a slipway, having some new plates fitted. In rolling seas the *Guendolen* attacked but the Victorian ammunition being used (by a volunteer gunner!) produced one dud shot in every four. Finally a hit was made and the German commander, furiously angry about the intrusion, came out to the *Guendolen*, was invited aboard, and immediately taken prisoner. His surprise was absolute since he had not been told that war had started. Even given that knowledge he would hardly have expected his friend, the captain of the *Guendolen*, to have given him such short shrift. The whole action seemed to be not quite cricket!

Because Karonga was so near to German occupied territory in what is now Tanzania, a force was quickly despatched from Zomba at the outset of the war in case the Germans invaded across the Songwe river. A huge hollow baobab tree was part of Karonga's fortifications. A gun platform was built in it with firing slits made through the trunk. The tree still stands with portions of the brickwork still visible.

From Karonga, British columns moved north, while German columns moved south and, travelling through the bush, they passed each other without realising it.

The Germans reached Karonga and attacked: then, after heavy fighting, withdrew. The noise of guns brought the Nyasaland force back and a hard battle – the Battle of Karonga – took place. There was tough fighting with heavy casualties on both sides. Eventually the Germans retreated over the border.

◀ *The spoils of war – sad relics of imperial might*

▼ *The beach at Karonga is now the scene of peaceful trading with nearby Tanzania*

▲ *Entrance to the old war graves cemetery at Karonga*

"O'er the shot-riddled wall of Karonga is flying
The flag of the Empire we fought to defend.
And low in the sand by Lake Nyasa are lying
The lads who were true to it, true to the end."

Robert Hellier Napier

Karonga was not attacked again but many troops marched through there on their way to fight in the prolonged East African Campaign. Of prime importance in the transport of stores over difficult terrain were thousands of *tenga tenga* or carriers, without whom the supply route could not have been kept open. Four and a half thousand of these men died, nearly all from disease.

Fort Johnston, now Mangochi, at the southern end of the lake was where the soldiers gathered for embarkation. Here, as at Karonga, there are war graves, though some of these soldiers in the south died not in war action but from the influenza epidemic in 1918.

People at the lake also became familiar with another branch of the forces, the Royal Flying Corps (R.F.C.). Maligned by some and made fun of by others, these pioneer aeroplanes and their crews made a valuable contribution to the war effort by providing photographs and reconnaissance reports and by dropping bombs. There was a homemade version of the latter, contrived from petrol tins, dynamite, stones, iron nuts and rusty nails. With this type of bomb under the plane and the main petrol tank under his seat, the observer experienced a perilous ride, as well as a cramped one when he had two spare tins of petrol between his legs!

There were great problems with the transport of spares and equipment and, because the aeroplanes were only capable of a minimal flying time, sometimes the planes had to be dismantled and loaded on a lake steamer to reach the vicinity of their destination.

Leo Walmsley, who flew in such planes over East Africa and Nyasaland, tells of one of his flights when the petrol pipe started to leak and the only way he could stop it was to staunch it with his hand. This led to the plane stalling and it came down in a maize field fourteen miles north of Malindi mission. Just as he was contemplating a long walk in the blazing sun, an African appeared on penny-farthing bicycle, much reinforced with bamboo, and allowed Walmsley the use of it to reach the mission.

Like oversized dragon-flies, with fabric wings stretched over wooden frames, these flimsy planes flew over the great bush areas of Africa, east and north of the lake. They and their crews were the forerunners of "the few" who forty years later would win the Battle of Britain.

Nyasa becomes Malawi

THE World Wars probably produced the first puffs of the winds of change which eventually blew the cobwebs of colonialism away.

Even in the first of those wars John Chilembwe had asked why black men should fight in white men's wars. It was one of many questions he asked concerning the status of Africans. He found no answers in the short-lived rebellion which ended in his death. But seeds were sown.

World War Two exposed even more Africans to the foibles and frailties of their rulers and when the Central African Federation was imposed in Nyasaland in the nineteen fifties, a gale-force storm of nationalism, led by Dr. H. Kamuzu Banda, refused to be quelled.

Nkhata Bay was the scene of a violent confrontation in 1959 when people died for their belief in the possibility of self-rule.

The people persisted in asking questions until they finally got the answer they wanted – Nyasaland would be given Independence.

And what name could the country possibly take but Malawi, a revival of that first Maravi. This time, however, 'Malawi' would encompass the length and breadth of the historic land.

◀ *Nkhata Bay, scene of a violent confrontation in the independence struggle*

▲ *John Chilembwe, photographed with his family in 1914*

◄ The Lake, since Livingstone's day known as Lake Nyasa and often the scene of suffering and war, would become Lake Malawi, background to a new era of peace.

The lake and its boats

PERHAPS the most peaceful picture, and certainly the most evocative among a visitor's photographs, is that of a dug-out canoe, silhouetted against the sunset on Lake Malawi.

These traditional dug-outs have been paddled on the lake for generations. They are skilfully fashioned with an adze-like tool and given a point of balance which enables a boat to roll up to ninety degrees on its side and yet recover. So, though the paddler appears to perch in a precarious position, in fact, if the boat is made with well-shaped in-curved lips, it is unlikely to overturn. The canoes are often made a long distance from the lake because of the need for specific trees, and even as far back as the last century people talked about following "canoe roads" to the lake.

Another romantic sight on the lake is that of a dhow with sail spread before the wind. Dhows were introduced by the Arabs, probably to cope with the growing slave trade in the middle of last century, when their beauty was sullied by the knowledge of their human cargo. Livingstone watched a dhow being built and was impressed by the boat builders. *"I should never think of carrying more than the engine and boilers of a vessel past the cataracts [on the Shire River]; the hull could be built here more easily than it could be conveyed".*

For his first exploration of the lake, Livingstone used a four-oared gig with a sail; it was only with the *Ilala* that steam made its debut. The *Ilala*, named after the district where Livingstone died, was made in Britain and transported in headloads past the Shire cataracts and rebuilt at the lake, where it was launched in 1875. This was some feat as

◄ *A dhow sails gracefully before the wind, symbol of a by-gone age*

▶ *Little removed from its original tree, a newly built canoe rests on its bed of chippings*

▲ *The m.v.* Sunbird *approaches Ilala Gap at Cape Maclear*

◄ *The present-day* Ilala *was launched in 1951 and makes a weekly round trip on the lake*

she weighed 21 tons when completed. A similar method was followed by the UMCA, the ALC and the Protectorate government when they transported, rebuilt and launched their boats.

Indeed, the country's history could well-nigh be plotted by a survey of the boats that have sailed on the lake-explorer's boats, mission boats, gun-boats, trading-cum-passenger boats and fishing boats, followed by the Lake Service as we know it today and resting for the moment with the lately launched *Kwacha*. This is the first container ship on the lake, tailor-made to assist imports and exports via the Lake/Northern Corridor route to Dar es Salaam.

Boats on the lake run the whole gamut, from canoes, through rowing, sailing and speed boats, for, given an

▼ *The dawn line-up in the Lake Malawi Yachting Marathon*

▶ *Nkopola Lodge, in the distance, is a favourite haunt of sailors*

expanse of water, man must needs travel over it, if not for business – then for pleasure.

The lake provides an idyllic situation for sailing and is popular with enthusiasts of all standards. In general, the conditions are excellent in terms of both weather and water temperature. The lake deserves considerable respect, however, as waves have been known to rise above four metres.

Most sailors prefer the cooler months when the *mwera*, a south-easterly wind blows up to thirty knots. The winds tend to be at their most challenging in July when the Lake Malawi Yachting Marathon is held. The race, which raises valuable funds for charity, is the longest of its kind in Africa with a course of 500km. Open to all classes of two man catamarans, the event attracts competitors from home and abroad who come to enjoy competitive sailing on one of nature's most inviting stretches of water.

▲ *Lakeshore basket-makers on the road to a nearby market with their brightly coloured wares*

▶ *The 'machila', not altogether popular among early visitors to Central Africa*

Comings and goings

VISITORS to Malawi are invariably struck by the sight of crowds of people coming and going on the roads. It is as though some primeval wanderlust seizes people; maybe it is an inheritance from their forefathers, who wandered far before they settled here. How they travel is immaterial; if all else fails they will walk. A similar attitude existed in Victorian England, so early visitors to Malawi saw no problem in covering long distances: in fact, Livingstone recommended walking as part of the cure for malaria.

Missionaries continued Livingstone's tradition of tramping over Africa. Bishop Smythies, who chose Likoma as the headquarters of the UMCA, talked of the delight of seeing friendly faces *"after a lonely walk of sixteen days across the forest"*. Reputed to be able to talk continuously while walking for miles, Smythies walked back to Zanzibar from the lake in forty-five days.

People who were unable or unwilling to walk made use of a *machila*, a sort of swinging, hammock-like contraption carried by a team of men, whose songs might or might not be complimentary to the person being carried. Not many travellers praised the *machila* and one referred to it as *"an invention of the devil"*. He gave the practical advice that the *machila* should be well off the ground and suggested that pillows or blankets should be placed in the *machila* *"especially when used by a lady, as serious damage may result from contact with a jagged stump"*.

Once wheels appeared in the country, bush carts were used, especially on estates. These consisted of a platform of wood with a seat, placed over a single motor-cycle wheel. Shafts before and behind were used for pushing and pulling rather than carrying. The *garetta*, which was rather like a rickshaw, had two wheels and was also pushed and pulled.

Most early travellers to the lake came up the Shire river by boat, travelled overland through Blantyre to avoid the Shire cataracts, and then rejoined the river at Matope. They took a river boat from Matope to Fort Johnston and then embarked on a lake boat.

◄ *Porters waiting for head-loads at ALC headquarters in Mandala, Blantyre*

▶ *A garetta. Much pride was taken in matching livery for the unfortunates who had to push and pull*

In 1891 Lionel Declé travelled on the *Domira, "a dirty little boat of about 80 tons. The only cabin consisted of a kind of cupboard with two bunks, this being considered proper accommodation for three passengers. Not that this mattered, for the cabin was so hot that it was impossible for anyone but a resolute suicide to sleep there."*

Another person referred disparagingly to the gun-boat *Guendolen* as a *"funny little boat ... really little bigger than a Durban tug".*

In spite of their shortcomings, these boats were sturdy and long-lasting. The *Guendolen* was only broken up in 1944 and the *Domira* launched in 1890, lasted until 1957 when it was deliberately sunk at Liwonde to close the gap in the new bund.

The record for endurance is held by the UMCA boat the *Chauncy Maples*, still working on the lake, now for Malawi Railways, ninety years after its launch, albeit in re-structured form.

Most routes between settlements, though graced by the name road, were merely tracks and even where a road was deliberately built, the result was not usually an easier way. Dr Laws engineered the Gorode escarpment road from the lakeshore up to Khondowe plateau but one of the missionaries said that travellers on it *"had to put a severe test on their vocabulary of adjectives to describe its difficulties"*.

Prior to World War One the only macadamised road was from Blantyre to Zomba and four wheeled vehicles were still fairly rare, but bicycles, and later motorcycles, became popular.

The war brought changes, as wars always do, and cars and box-bodies began to be available for those who could afford them. Visits to the lakeshore became more frequent.

In the 1930s a railway extension was made from Blantyre to Salima, connecting with lake services at Chipoka. This brought public transport to the lake.

◄ *The Gorode escarpment road toils up the shoulder of the Rift Valley to Livingstonia in 19 tortuous bends*

90

◄ *The flying boats of BOAC's African service 'landed' in the sheltered bay of Golden Sands at Cape Maclear*

▲ *The Cape Maclear Hotel served passengers on the flying boat service for only one year, 1949/50*

The first aeroplanes seen at the lake were probably military planes, one of which crashed at Malindi in 1916. In 1926 a French flying boat came down at Fort Johnston and in 1928 Sir Alan Cobham also arrived by flying boat. He intended to come down at Karonga but was not sure if the water would be deep enough, so used the lake off Vua instead. He next came down at Fort Johnston. His purpose was to seek financial support for his proposed flying boat service to South Africa but the administration of the day turned the chance down. There was a long wait before any civil aviation serviced the lakeshore, though landing strips were made in main settlements for light aircraft. After World War Two civil aviation began to develop.

These were the days of leisurely travel, even when travelling by air. A perfect example of this was the flying boat service. Already functioning to South Africa, it was finally decided in 1949 to include Nyasaland in the scheme and have a flying boat service calling at Cape Maclear.

At that time there was already a 'luxury' hotel at Cape Maclear, with a swimming pool and golf course. There was a landing strip there for light aircraft. Originally most people and supplies arrived by boat: but by the time the hotel was fully opened travellers and goods could arrive by road, – when weather conditions were good.

BOAC (British Overseas Airways Corporation) started a weekly service by flying boat in November 1949. The flight on a Short Solent took three and a half days from Cape Maclear to Southampton, each night being spent at a hotel en route. The plane held 28 passengers and had two decks where passengers could either observe the country over which they were flying, or stun themselves with cocktails. It was elegant but painfully slow when compared with the new jet airliner, the Comet, which had recently appeared. The Comet changed travel forever. The idea of the journey being part of the holiday was removed and replaced by all the ravages of jet-lag and facile mottoes such as *"Time is Money"*, when we all know that time is priceless.

▲ *The new Southern Lakeshore air-strip has greatly facilitated transfers to the hotels near Mangochi and is served regularly by the national airline, Air Malawi*

◀ *A BOAC 'Solent' flying-boat arrives at Cape Maclear*

After one year the Flying Boat Service closed down. Perhaps it was never practical, but it was certainly romantic!

Since that time of course the absolute decline of international sea travel has been seen. In its place there is fast air travel which brings in tourists and travellers from all over the world, with most visitors to Malawi preferring to fly to Lilongwe or Blantyre and then continuing to the lake by road or air.

A very practical idea was the lakeshore road conceived in the sixties and completed to gravel standard in the 1970s. Stretching from Mangochi in the south to Karonga in

◄ *The beautiful 'Corniche' style road which runs from Mzuzu down to the lakeshore at Chiweta*

▲ *Looking down on the same road before the steep drop to Chiweta*

▼ *The m.v.* Ilala, *sturdy work-horse of the Lake Service, was launched at Monkey Bay in 1951*

the north, this road now in the final stages of upgrading to full tar, has opened up the whole lakeshore for visitors and residents alike. It includes sections like that on the escarpment above Chiweta a beautiful road from both scenic and engineering points of view.

Not all road problems have disappeared, however. Sometimes harsh, tropical storms cause flooding and broken bridges and leave behind pot-holes and many unpaved roads remain. However, the man who earlier this century complained that African travel tries every quality a man possesses – *"temper, teeth, tact, patience, purse and perseverance"* – would have to retract his words (or most of them!) in modern Malawi.

Public transport on the lake has always been of prime importance to Malawi.

Just as World War Two was ending, a new ship, the *Vipya*, was nearing completion at Monkey Bay. She was the biggest boat yet to appear on the lake with a displacement of 470 tons and was meant to cater as a lake transport for people who travelled the lake by necessity and at the same time to offer a comfortable means for tourists to travel the lake. She came to a tragic end – one might almost say a sad beginning – because on her third scheduled trip she sank during a storm, with the loss of 145 lives, almost all those on board. Among the many questions raised about the cause of the disaster – was it due to the weather, human miscalculation or an ill-balanced boat? – one fact was sure: the Lake Service was bereft of its new boat. The whole process had to start again.

▼ *The* Ilala *leaves Monkey Bay on her weekly voyage around the lake*

▶ *A trip on the* Ilala *is a memorable experience and emphasises the immensity of Lake Malawi*

ILALA
MONKEY BAY

In 1951 the replacement boat, the m.v. *Ilala II*, was launched. Somewhat larger than the *Vipya*, she has been a successful boat, fulfilling her bread and butter work and also carrying visitors the length of the lake in comfort.

To travel on the *Ilala II* is probably the only way to get a completely satisfying picture of the immensity of Lake Malawi. Calls at remote settlements and ports introduce in a unique way the diversity of people, scenery and life on this great inland sea.

▲ *The huge sugar estate and mill at Dwangwa also produces, in a separate plant, ethanol which serves as a valuable import substitute*

▶ *The crocodile farm at Dwanga is one of several on the lakeshore*

Lake life in the nineties

SINCE the watershed of Malawi's Independence, life in lakeshore settlements has been directed to take on a new impetus. Bewitched by the lake's soporific charms, and not overwhelmed by offers of aid, some colonial servants opted for an *"unspoilt"* policy which sometimes meant undeveloped. The new Malawi had to choose where to build on existing resources and where to invest anew.

Much effort has been focused on special regional schemes and on Rural Growth centres. The Rural Growth Centres concentrate on community services. They provide a nucleus of services needed by any community: dispensary, primary school, market, post-office, community hall and agricultural extension services. Ideally these centres should make life easier and more attractive to lakeside dwellers and so help to stop aimless drifting to towns.

Regional agricultural schemes and private estates provide new job opportunities. The sugar scheme at Dwangwa, north of Nkhotakota on the mid-west lakeshore is a big post-independence project and involves not only the production of sugar but also an ethanol plant where fuel is produced from sugar waste. There is also a small crocodile farm there. Rice growing, first introduced by the Swahili people, now flourishes in rice schemes in the Nkhotakota, Salima and Karonga areas. Cotton grows well in the Salima area, while tea, rubber and macadamia nuts are grown in the Nkhata Bay district. On the lakeside plains there is of course mixed farming, with maize and groundnut growing and livestock. The high irrigation potential of the lakeshore is very under-exploited while wind and solar power is still in its infancy.

Wind and water together could easily provide wave pumps for crop irrigation given a huge lake with a tide-like effect caused by passful winds.

Fluctuations in lake level, apparently occurring in cycles, caused great social upheaval as recently as 1979. Whole villages like Mponda's had to resettle on higher ground when the lake level rose. Some holiday cottages were ruined and lakeshore hotels found the fishing a bit too close for comfort.

At such times perhaps the only consolation is rice cropped from flooded areas.

Cottage craft industries abound, weaving being most noticeable. Once the lake road levels out from the southern highlands, ranks of chief chairs are left behind and their place is taken by a multitude of woven goods.

Oblong sleeping mats, oval door mats, hang near colourful round floor mats of soft woven grass, and others heavy with plaited coils, ready for cool polished concrete floors.

Laundry baskets stand like Ali Baba pots and carry cots of ample proportions lie waiting to be frilled, quilted or decorated as desired.

Closer to the lake are stands of hats, row after row of them, natty trilbies, handsome stetsons, wide sombreros and the ultimate beach comber's hat with long fringed edges, as though someone started it and then couldn't be bothered to finish. Toys line up on the dusty earth. These are also made from basket work but with well-deserved detail adding novelty – car bonnets that lift up, Land Rovers with spare wheels and helicopters with blades that turn while doll's furniture echoes the full-size verandah furniture also on sale.

Large baskets of great variety provide an overwhelming choice and small ones nestle inside each other like sets of Russian dolls.

There is immense satisfaction to be had from these mementos, keepsakes which, even when carried far from the lake, will still retain woven into them, the timeless flavour of life 'at the Lake'.

◀ *Rubber thrives in the high rainfall area south of Nkhata Bay*

▼ *The lakeshore craftsmen are very inventive with raw materials such as seeds, grass and bamboo; here a* bawo *seller*

◀ *The vast sugar fields at Dwanga*

104

The shining harvest

WHATEVER new harvests are gathered from the land in lakeshore areas, the perennial shining harvest of the lake itself is a vital mainstay of life in Malawi. Fish provide a high percentage of all animal protein eaten here and the fishing industry offers employment to thousands.

The immense depth of the northern lake – up to 700 metres – with a subsequent lack of oxygen, prohibits life, so in fact size for size the lake is less productive than some other lesser lakes in Malawi such as Lake Chilwa. Nevertheless the concentration and variety of fish at the southern end of the lake contributes a great deal of the country's total catch.

The largest commercial fishery is Maldeco which continues a business founded over forty years ago. There is also a number of other smaller fisheries. At Maldeco fish are trawled, processed, frozen and distributed from there to markets all over Malawi.

◄ *The dawn catch*

▲ *A temporary fishing settlement right on the beach*

Traditional village fishing techniques also include seine-netting, ring-netting, gill-netting and traps. Fishermen follow the fish and very large fishing camps can be seen along the lakeshore. Many canoes are still used but plank boats are favoured when affordable because they can carry bigger loads more safely. Similarly, people who can afford machine-made nets use them instead of hand-made ones.

▲ *Trawling brings large hauls of* chambo

◄ *On board the m.v.* Crystal Lake

▶ *Traditional fish drying in Chembe Village, Cape Maclear*

◄ *Homeward bound*

Fishing for *usipa* is done at night when fish are attracted to the surface by lights and are caught in seine-nets.

Some of the huge harvest is preserved by sun-drying but mostly it is smoked in the lake villages. Once dried, the fish travels to town in trucks, piled high in pick-ups or in baskets on bicycles. Recently an ice-plant has been installed at Mangochi and if this is successful others will no doubt follow and more fresh fish can then be sold in towns.

Kampango, caught and smoked commercially, is a popular delicacy but probably the most popular fish is *chambo*, a favourite with both residents and visitors.

Much employment is generated, not only for people who actually do the fishing, but also for those who build boats, repair engines and make nets.

As well as the food harvest the lake also provides thousands of aquarium fish, in particular those of the *Cichlidae* family many of which are only found in Lake Malawi. This business is of great economic importance.

The fish industry as a source of life and wealth to the country is protected by government regulations. These aim to stop the illegal catching of immature fish, which would lead to a gradual depletion of stock.

The Lake gives life to Malawi; the Lake deserves the protection afforded to it.

◀ *Tending the nets*

▲ *Some of the colourful* cichlids *for which the lake is famous*

▲ *A fishing village just north of Mangochi*

▶ *The Shire River drains Lake Malawi first into Lake Malombe*

116

Lake settlements

FACILITIES in the major settlements around the lakeshore have been improved with new or up-graded schools, hospitals, post-offices and administration centres, yet most places are still at a fairly rural stage. Until the lakeshore road was built, communications along the lakeshore were poor, which is probably an underlying reason for lack of economic growth in the littoral.

Mangochi, originally a military post with a harbour for gun-boats and a boat-building centre, looked set to become a major town, but it lost its *"raison d'etre"* when the river became too low for boat travel and the railway extension was routed to another part of the lake. Now it is even by-passed by the road to the southern lakeshore hotels. Nevertheless Mangochi is well worth a visit.

Founded by Sir Harry Johnston in 1891 whilst he was trying to subdue recalcitrant chiefs and slavers, it was first built on the east bank of the Shire river. Fort Johnston, as it was then called, was built for tactical reasons opposite the heavily populated Mponda's village. It was surrounded by a moat of stagnant water, which lay below river level. Given the mosquitoes that abound in that area, there is little wonder that malaria and blackwater fever took a heavy toll. By 1897, when the Fort's military needs had been diminished by the successful repression of the slave trade, a new settlement was made to the west of the river.

▲ *Before the bridge at Mangochi was built in 1976, the ferry was the only way of reaching the eastern lakeshore*

◄ *Shortly after leaving the lake, the Shire narrows at Mangochi – at the start of its 300 mile journey to the Indian Ocean*

Mangochi was declared a township in 1899 and early this century had a hotel and a yacht club, started by Sir Alfred Sharpe, who also helped plan the town. The yacht club is now long defunct but its premises are used as a Lakeshore Museum.

The museum, which is being rehabilitated, has sections on the life of lakeshore people and on the fish, flora and fauna of the area. There is also a section devoted to some of the old lake boats, including a few fitments salvaged in 1970 from the *Queen Victoria* after 25 years under the lake water. The good working condition of these parts and the absence of any corrosion illustrates well the purity of the lake water.

The Hotchkiss gun, used on the *Guendolen* in World War One can be seen near Kamuzu Bridge, while nearby is the Queen Victoria Memorial Clock Tower and the Vipya Memorial Plaque.

Once across the bridge (which replaced a ferry in 1976) the road soon divides with one road climbing to the hill country. Here, overlooking tobacco farms, are Mangochi Mountain and the remains of Fort Mangochi. For people who enjoy a bracing climb this makes an interesting visit to a historic site.

◀ *The Queen Victoria Memorial Tower and the m.v.* Vipya *Memorial stand by the bridge in Mangochi*

The lower lakeshore road leads first to Malindi. Because of the height of Gome Mountain and the hills behind Malindi, the seasonal wind known as the *vuma* strikes the lake well away from the shore, thus leaving a sheltered mooring for vessels. It was for this reason that the Universities Mission to Central Africa (UMCA) used Malindi as a calling place and eventually set up a mission station there. David Livingstone passed through here on his last journey: *"we pushed close to the lake by Mt. Gome"*. There is a church, St. Martin's, designed by Frank George, the architect of Likoma Cathedral. There are also other old mission buildings and a pottery which was established in the late 1970s.

◄ *Palm trees are prolific in Mangochi at the southern end of the lake. Coconuts are sold commonly by the roadside here*

The road continues past Malindi to Makanjila, with its Rural Growth Centre, and then on to Fort Maguire. Nothing remains of the first Fort, which was originally built on the lakeshore and named after Captain Maguire a former Military-Commandant who was killed there in 1891, or of the fort which was later rebuilt on higher ground. Just north of Fort Maguire is the border with Mozambique.

The whole of Lake Malawi was Nyasaland territory until 1950. At that time an agreement was made whereby in exchange for £100,000 towards a survey of the drainage of the Shire Valley, Mozambique gained about 2,780 square miles of the lake.

▲ *Hippos laze by the Shire River. They are often seen in the more remote parts of the lake*

◄ *The original boiler of the Chauncy Maples lies on the beach at Malindi where the vessel was first built over ninety years ago*

North from Mangochi on the west side of the River Shire is Mponda's, a big, old village. Chief Mponda was far from helpful to the early Protectorate government. A. J. Swann tells how the chief caused a large tree to be thrown over the river to block navigation, while his people stood on the shore pointing their flintlock guns at Swann and the others in the *Lady Nyasa*. The Captain of the boat suggested that all on board should stand at the stern of the boat and then *"as the ship mounted the tree, the Captain shouted run [forward] as fast as you can. We did, and the little craft struggled over, with a heavy list into deep water on the other side. This was marine steeple-chasing ... In those days no-one stood at trifles. Things had to be done."*

Monkey Bay with its beautiful natural harbour is headquarters of the Malawi Railways Lake Service. It is strange that the harbour was little used in the early days. Gradually its advantages began to be appreciated and now it is the terminus for the *Ilala II*, *Mtendere* and *Chauncy Maples* passenger ships and also for cargo boats. The boats are serviced in the dockyards and dry dock here.

Monkey Bay as a settlement is smaller than anyone ever expects with just the bare necessities of a small supermarket, service station, post office and a dry-season landing strip.

◀ *Monkey Bay nestles in one of the most captivating settings and is the headquarters of the Lake Service*

▲ *The beach at Malindi*

Between Mponda's and Monkey Bay, and including the diversion to Cape Maclear (called Samlio in pre-Livingstone days), the lakeshore is dotted with various hotels, resorts, and holiday cottages, which intermingle happily with fishing villages and fisheries. Beach after beach, in scenic bays or on stretches of palm-fringed shore, invite the visitor to one of the last luxuries in a crowded world – the luxury of space.

◀ *Malawi's beaches are never over-crowded with holiday makers.*

127

▲ The quaint rest-house on the beach at Nkhotakota utilises in its construction much of the detritus of marine engineering

▶ Nkhotakota is redolent of the lake's colourful past with many reminders of its brushes with history

The lake road continues north passing the busy railhead and port of Chipoka and the small but growing town of Salima, with its stores, market, government offices and dry-season airstrip.

Another smaller resort area lies about 20km from Salima at Senga Bay.

Nkhotakota once reputed to be the largest village in Central Africa and notorious in the last century for its slave trade, is the next sizeable settlement. There is a strong Islamic influence here and the long arab style robe, named *khanzu* in Swahili, is much in evidence, making a picturesque scene reminiscent of the East African coast.

The UMCA was active there from the 1890s and the mission station was built around the "Livingstone tree", where Livingstone is recorded as having had discussions with the local chief. *"We arrived at Kota-kota Bay in the afternoon of the 10th September, 1863, and sat down under a magnificent wild fig-tree with leaves ten inches long by five broad, about a quarter of a mile from the village of Juma ben Saidi. ... Juma, who is evidently the chief person here ... came to salute us."* In fact two fig trees are preserved in the town, both fitting the description and the distance from the chief's original village, quoted by Livingstone: one at the UMCA Mission and the other on the road to the mosque on the shore.

▶ *The view from the dramatic escarpment road toward Mlowe*

▶▶ *The beach at Chintheche is one of the most attractive on the whole lakeshore*

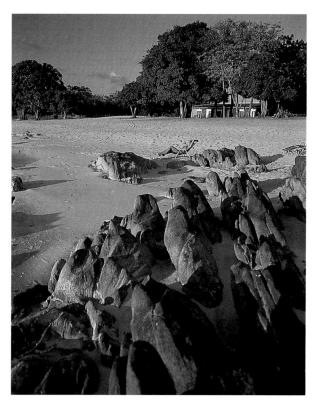

The church at the mission was designed by Frank George. Bishop Chauncy Maples, who was drowned in the lake shortly after becoming Bishop, is buried there.

Distance from the main towns of the central and southern regions is probably the reason why the northern lakeshore has never attracted a large influx of visitors. With better roads to Mzuzu and the tarring of the lakeshore road nearing completion, more people are lured to places like Chintheche, with its superfine beach. A number of rest-houses are also appearing in bays to the north of Nkhata Bay, probably the start of the "resort area" on the northern lakeshore.

At Nkhata Bay, according to discerning Malawian residents "probably" the prettiest of Lake Malawi's bays, the road has to swing inland because the way is blocked by mountains, which drop precipitously to lake level. The road curls round to the lake again and down the impressive Chiweta escarpment, which gives panoramic views over the northern lake, and towards Manchewe Falls near Livingstonia Mission.

Chilumba port, journey's end for most lake travellers, is assuming growing importance in the "Northern Corridor" system. It has recently been rehabilitated with the addition of bigger fuel and cargo handling facilities and a longer jetty. It can now handle 180,000 metric tons of goods per year and is an important link in Malawi's import and export chain through Dar es Salaam. Facilities for shopping and accommodation are still fairly minimal.

Karonga, in the area where the dinosaurs started it all, is only now beginning to evolve as one might have expected. Attempts last century to open a way – the Stevenson Road – to Lake Tanganyika, never amounted to much and ultimately the southern route into the country became the popular way. So Karonga's growth was slow but steady like many of the other lakeshore settlements and its main thrust of rebuilding and re-siting initially came more as a result of lake flooding than of natural growth.

◄ *Chilumba port has been specially constructed as part of the Northern Corridor facility*

Shifts in the political scene in countries surrounding Malawi have put the spotlight on the northern route to the sea via Dar es Salaam, with a consequent rise in the importance of Karonga. Under the Secondary Centres Development Programme, construction of a new Karonga township has begun. There will be a new town centre, new civic offices, market, bus station and craft centre.

With the full opening of the Northern Corridor, Karonga, situated in an important position at one end of the Karonga-Ibanda road, may well turn into the mini-metropolis people once expected.

▶ *The main Karonga beach*

▶▶ *The pots have just arrived by dugout from Tanzania*

134

"Karonga! Never more thy fate to be
Nought but an outpost on a distant lake."

Rober Hellier Napier

▶ *The scenic road from the Monkey Bay turn-off to Cape Maclear twists and turns through beautiful woodland within the Lake Malawi National Park*

▶▶ *This sign outside Mango-chi disappeared with the building of the road to Monkey Bay but elephants have recently been sighted again at the Southern Lakeshore*

The Lake and its visitors

WATER means life for man. Maybe it is this sub-conscious knowledge that draws people to water for relaxation. Certainly Malawi's Great Water never disappoints and lures people back time and time again.

When Livingstone returned to the lake during his last journey he felt great joy: *"It was as if I had come back to an old home I never expected to see again, and it was pleasant to bathe in the delicious water once more, or hear the roar of the sea and dash in the rollers..."*

A similar delight was felt by all who came under the lake's spell and early visitors defied the lakeside mosquitoes in their search for relaxation and holiday.

By the turn of the century a hotel was established at Fort Johnston (now Mangochi). As time passed, other places on the lakeshore provided competition. By the mid-nineteen thirties, with a railway extension to the lake at Chipoka, the Salima area became popular, with three hotels – the Lake Nyasa Hotel, the Lake Shore Hotel and the Grand Beach Hotel – all vying for trade.

By then Monkey Bay also had a hotel (two pounds per week, full board!) and, in the dry season anyway, they could claim *"Road perfect right through"*.

At the same time Fort Johnston had the "Fort Road House" and advertised good duck shooting. The 1940's saw a hotel at Cape Maclear with good, though short-lived, prospects of flying boat trade.

The hotels had varied fortunes. Most changed hands and changed names; some kept their names and lost their

reputation; some were taken down and built elsewhere while others fell down and were not resurrected. Through all these fortunes, good and bad, there was always the underlying knowledge that Lake Malawi was an ideal holiday area, just waiting to be "discovered".

With modern advertising and modern communications the dreams of the early hoteliers begin to come true, though visitors can rejoice that so far Malawi has escaped the kind of influx that, simply by being there, spoils what it set out to enjoy.

◀ *Golden Sands at Cape Maclear, long favoured site for major hotel development, is also favoured by the builders of 'lake cottages'*

A lake for the future?

Now when mankind has been awakened from a deep sleep of ignorance; when we begin to realise the frailty of resources we once thought everlasting; now in the eleventh hour of *"laissez-faire"*, we take a new look at Lake Malawi. Like a man living on borrowed time we begin to appreciate its wealth and diversity, its beauty and its life.

142

Visitors to the lake are impressed by the variety of vegetation. From different seasons and different locations, memories will flood the mind:

The ghostly green of fever trees; a flaming *erythrina* brightening up the bush; puffs of white fluff beneath the kapok trees; the gigantic sausage-shaped fruit of the *kigelia* and its equally striking, blowsy crimson flowers. Remember the boabab, dinosaur of trees with its velvety fruits; palms, indigenous and imported – oil palm, coconut palm, ivory palm; stately ebonies; cassias and flamboyants in the town streets, and wild figs, some of which insinuate themselves round other trees and celebrate the strangulation by giving deep shade and pretending they were always there.

In the lush green of the wet season, mangoes proliferate while the pale, crackling, leafless twigs of the dry season are festooned here and there with strings of red, pink and white flowering creepers.

Birds are equally memorable. Drawn in bold, distinctive shapes, so that even the least knowledgeable can recognise them, are pelicans, hamerkops, cormorants, kingfishers, egrets and fish-eagles. Observe these birds while

◄ *Egrets on a sausage tree*

◄◄ *Dark green mango trees stand guardian along many of Lake Malawi's fine beaches*

they sit, still as rocks, watching for food. No flitter-flutter here. Just a silent sitting, hovering and swooping, then cries of triumph. Who could ever forget the cry of Malawi's fish-eagle, bold, wild and a complete celebration of freedom?

And how accommodating of the weaver birds to put on house building displays, discarding their misshapes so that with their conscience clear you can inspect their meticulous work.

Birdlife at the lake is rich and colourful and if some birds flash past, merely colour strokes, how comforting to have such names as "lilac-breasted roller" to toss around your tongue and say "I'm sure it was".

There is a world of insects at the lake too: iridescent dragon-flies; may-flies that dance and mate and die; furry moths; kaleidoscopic butterflies, and fire-flies that spangle the night. Other insects are remembered less for their gauzy wings than for their troublesome habits: mosquitoes that leave you with malaria, mputze flies that, given half a chance, hatch their young beneath your skin, and clouds of lake flies that swarm round lamps, and rain on you and even permeate mosquito netting. It takes all sorts to make an insect world.

◄◄ *The fish eagle concentration along the southern shores of the lake is the densest in Africa*

◄ *Cormorants at guano splashed Boadzulu Island, opposite the southern lakeshore hotels*

146

The number of animals has diminished. Heavy population pressure has changed the face of the lakeshore, which must once have resembled a giant water-hole. *"Down to the lake during the night all sorts of antelopes, big and small, had come to drink, leaving the track of their footprints in the sand."* That was in 1895. In much more recent times, we were advised on the lakeshore road *"Beware of Elephants"*; now we have to beware of goats and cattle!

Even so there are still many wild animals and reptiles. Otters perform their aquabatics for lucky visitors and giant monitor lizards bask in the sun on Boadzulu Island. Hippos maintain their territory even near lake cottages and hotels. On the one hand they snort and guffaw engagingly for visitors while on the other they wreak havoc with village crops and trample down anybody, villager or visitor, who gets between them and their destination. Crocodiles take a toll that only slightly decreases year by year, and in adverse years, lions move down to feed at the cattle pens of the eastern lakeshore villages.

◀ *A monitor lizard among lake-washed rocks*

◀◀ *Beautiful behemoths! Hippos flirt with the photographer*

148

As early as the 1920s some birds were already protected and in the 1930's wise and far-seeing laws protected whole sections of the lakeshore. In 1954 part of the Nkhotakota area became Nkhotakota Game Reserve. Protected and reserved. Put the words together and get "Preserved". That is the real aim, to preserve the area as it is, unspoilt, undeveloped, unexploited. Visitors are allowed there if they are willing to take their own requirements with them and if they are willing to blend with the landscape, so that they become just another (temporary) species, privileged for a while to be part of the scene.

Also being protected is the area centred at Cape Maclear and known as Lake Malawi National Park.

The offshore islands and part of the mainland were first protected in the 1930s but a new and quite breathtaking concept is that of preserving the actual water of the lake and the marine life in it, up to 100 metres from the shore. The National Park, which covers an area of 140km² and enjoys a large population and many visitors, presents more difficult problems than a place like Nkhotakota Game Reserve. Here at Cape Maclear villagers and holiday-makers alike have to co-exist with nature without spoiling it.

A certain pride in the area is growing since the Park was declared a World Heritage Centre in 1984. An educational complex has been built to try to ensure that future citizens of Malawi appreciate this unique area.

◄ *The islands around Monkey Bay benefit from protection within the Lake Malawi National Park*

▼ *The entrance road to the Lake Malawi National Park*

▼ *Mwalawamphini, 'rock of tribal markings', the pattern chiselled out by the cut and thrust of time and erosion*

▲ Otter Point at Cape Maclear, where some of the clearest water reveals a multitude of coloured mbuna

David Livingstone and John Kirk saw and remarked on the number and variety of fish when they visited Cape Maclear in the last century. Today's visitor has the advantage of being able to use snorkels and diving equipment and swim among these fish underwater, or to observe them from a specially designed boat with glass viewing panels. With over 500 and maybe as many as 1 000 species of fish in the whole lake and with 350 species occurring nowhere else in the world, Lake Malawi is indeed unique. Observers are amazed by the variety of brilliant colours and by the enormous numbers of fish swimming and grazing around the underwater boulders of Cape Maclear.

On land in the Lake Malawi National Park there is a variety of animals – duiker, bush-buck, klipspringer, leopard, bush-pig, porcupine and zebra – but most of them are timid and keep well out of the way, because only a short time ago this was a popular hunting area.

The wealth of scenery, the diversity of life, the laws of preservation are all a great inheritance. But there is also a debit side. At the southern end of the lake particularly, near heavily populated areas, are lands almost devoid of trees. Skimpy scrub only just holds its own as the sandy soil begins to resemble desert. In other areas deforestation has led to erosion and a sad change in landscape. Is man in his frailty and selfishness going to change, and change for the worse, what has lain unchanged for centuries? This is not a simple problem with simple answers. How do people cook food without wood? How do people make bricks without wood? How do people smoke fish without wood? These are the problems government grapples with as it takes steps to find alternative fuels.

▲ *The timelessness of life at the lake*

Meanwhile the message goes out: *"Cherish what you have; it is your only world, your only chance. The glory of Lake Malawi must be preserved."*

A last look

STAND on the beach at sunset, with shadows lying long across the sand and the opposite hills awash with the eerie green of the afterglow.

A last molten streak touches the lapping waves and the sky is layered with turquoise, rose and indigo.

An old tree stump juts from the water a few feet from the shore – there is always an old tree stump! – where a cormorant poses.

A big boat disgorges its catch and catchers, including many small boys, who tramp back along the sand to their village. They have their hands full, plastic bags full, even a straw hat full of little shining fishes.

They return your greeting with a smile, a nod, a raised hand. Here you are not just watching a scene in some antiseptic, sterile playground; for a moment you are part of their life, part of the living lake.

The sun gives a last touch to the marsh green meadow where egrets parade. The waves ripple softly in, while the magic of Lake Malawi enfolds you.

A fish-eagle screams goodnight.

Goodnight – but not goodbye!

Bibliography

Anderson-Morshead, A.E.M. History of the Universities' Mission to Central Africa (London 1955)

Antiquities, Dept. of, Heritage of Malawi (Blantyre 1989)

Ballantyne, M.M.S. & Shepherd, R.H.W. Forerunners of Modern Malawi (Lovedale 1968)

Baker, C.A. Johnston's Administration (Blantyre 1970)

Barnes, B.H. Johnson of Nyasaland (London 1933)

Boeder, Robert B. Alfred Sharpe of Nyasaland – Builder of Empire (Blantyre 1980)

Carter, Judy Malawi Wildlife, Park and Reserves (London 1987)

Cole-King, Paul Cape Maclear (Zomba 1968)

Cole-King, Paul Mangochi – The Mountain, the People and the Fort (Zomba 1972)

Cole-King, Paul Lake Malawi Steamers (Zomba 1971)

Copley, Hugh When Dragons Roamed East Africa (Nairobi 1948)

Coupland, Sir Reginald Kirk on the Zambesi (Oxford 1928)

Debenham, Frank Nyasaland – Land of the Lake (London 1955)

Dixey, F. The Nyasaland Section of the Great Rift Valley (Geographical Journal, August 1926)

Dixey, F. The Dinosaur Beds of Lake Nyasa (Transactions of the Royal Society of South Africa Vol. XVI Part I)

Drummond, Henry Tropical Africa (London 1888)

Foskett, Reginald (Ed.) The Zambesi Journals and Letters of Dr John Kirk (London 1965)

Fotheringham, L. Monteith Adventures in Nyassaland (London 1891, reprinted Blantyre 1986)

Garland Vera Lady of the Lake – The Story of the m.v. Chauncy Maples on Lake Malawi (Blantyre 1990)

Gelfand, Michael Lakeside Pioneers (Oxford 1964)

Hetherwick. A. (Ed.) Robert Hellier Napier in Nyasaland

Hine, J.E. Days Gone By (London 1924)

Hough, John Malawi's National Parks and Game Reserves (Blantyre 1989)

Howson, P.J. A Short History of Karonga (Zomba 1972)

Johnson, W.P. My African Reminiscences (London 1924)

Johnston, Sir H.H. British Central Africa (London 1897)

Linden, Ian (Ed.) Mponda Mission Diary (Lilongwe 1989)

Listowel, Judith The Other Livingstone (London 1974)

Livingstone, David & Charles The Zambesi & its Tributaries (London 1865)

Livingstone, W.P. Laws of Livingstonia (London 1921)

Maples, E. Chauncy Maples – Bishop of Likoma (London 1898)

Martin, C.G.C. Maps & Surveys of Malawi (Cape Town 1980)

Maurel, Martine Visitor's Guide to Malawi (Johannesburg 1990)

Mills, D.Y. What we do in Nyasaland (London 1911)

Pachai, B. The Early History of Malawi (London 1972)

Pachai, B. Malawi: The History of the Nation (London 1973)

Randolph, B.W. Arthur Douglas – The Story of his Life (London 1920)

Ransford, Oliver Livingstone's Lake (London 1966)

Surveys, Dept of The National Atlas of Malawi (Blantyre 1982)

Swann, Alfred J. Fighting the Slave Hunters in Central Africa (London 1910)

Tattersall D. The Land of the Lake (Blantyre 1982)

Walmsley, Leo Flying & Sport in East Africa (London 1920)

Ward, Gertrude Life of Bishop Smythies (London 1898)

Young, E.D. The Search After Livingstone (London 1868)

Young, E.D. Nyassa – A Journal of Adventure (London 1877)

Society of Malawi Journals